Navika Deol
Thinking and Feeling

The book

Head in clouds, my mind
far, far away …
guess it's poetry,
again, they say?
Again, I reply,
dive in or let it be,
it's up to you,
I invite you to be part of
this world in the clouds
or even on the ground?

The author

Navika Deol, born 1998 in Pforzheim, grew up with reading. She published her first book "Gedankenverloren" in 2018. "Thinking and Feeling" is her sixth book. She spends her free time with books, films, activism and on her blog, which can be found at: www.szebrabooks.de.

Thinking and Feeling

Navika Deol

Bibliographic information from the German National Library: The German National Library lists this publication in the German National Bibliography; detailed bibliographical data can be found on the internet at dnb.dnb.de

First Edition published in Germany

©2022 Navika Deol
Cover design: Navika Deol
Editors: Roman Hambrecht, Niels Ritzler
Author photo by Navika Deol
Illustrations by Navika Deol

Production and publishing:
BoD - Books on Demand, Norderstedt
ISBN: 978-3-7568-8815-3

For you and only you. I thought I'd never dedicate you a book. Turns out I was wrong.

For all the lovers and dreamers out there.

I think of you in my sleep
wishing you were here
right beside me …
… the image slowly fades
fades far, far away …
blurry lines
colour getting lost in water
slowly fading away …
Awake. Still thinking of you.
Doing everything wrong.
Wanting you to see me the way –
the way I see you.
In all those colours
exploding like feelings
feeling I can't hide anymore.
Wish you were here
right by my side …

Constantly thinking 'bout you –
wishing we could go to Paris and
have that cup of coffee
near the Tour Eiffel …
Not to forget:
have those long,
long walks at the Seine.
Your hand in mine,
sun already setting.
Grabbing glasses of red, red wine and
candlelight dinner
turning into moonlight dinner.
I see your silhouette,
our eyes meet.
You grab my hands and
pull me into the water.
Cold, but not that cold …
'cause you're by my side …
your warming body,
your lovely words.
I feel so blessed,
I'm so in love.

I'm in this state of mind.
Slowly fading away.
From everything and everyone
without anyone noticing.
Try to hold on but …
… I can't.
Strength has left me.
I'm all alone
surrounded by all these people.
Rushing feet, stressed faces.
Fast world, fast people.
I fade further.
Standing here,
in-between all of them,
slowly, slowly fading away.
A single tear drop –
 the rest? run dry.
I don't feel anymore.
I wish I could but
all gone
Faded away.
I begin to fall apart.

At night
you're in my head,
in my dreams,
in my mind.
Can't sleep
thinking 'bout you.
Thinking 'bout
telling you
how much I love you –
but I can't.
This pain, tears
keeping me awake …
… wishing you were here …
… wish I could be with you,
I miss you –
miss you so much
it hurts so bad …
miss you so much
'cause I love you?

Who could've told
I'd fall for you
fall so bad,
bad in love
with
every fibre of my body …
don't know what to do
what to feel
what to say …
feels like
the air is getting thinner
when I'm with you.

What if it was never
meant to be?
What if it was just
by chance we met?
What if we were not
meant to fall for each other?
And what if we actually
fell for one another?
What if? What if? What if?

And in this other life
we might meet again …
… as strangers, friends or even
lovers?
You tell me, tell me
how you feel,
how you wanna feel …
in this other life
everything might be different
or still the same?
Tell me what you'd prefer …
or even tell me
what you feel, now,
in this life and maybe,
maybe we get to be these
long lost lovers
finding each other after
having searched for eternity …
tell me one thing:
will it be this life or the next?

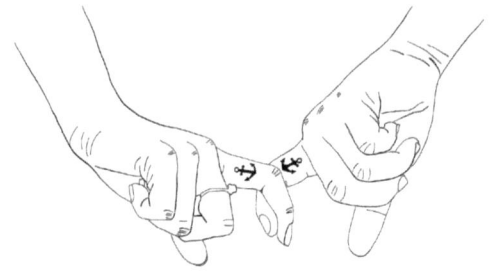

Meet me in the afterlife, she said,
she said before she went,
went away and didn't return.
Eyes closed, cold body …
… I'm taking my last breath,
feels like flying is what I say,
what I say before I go,
go and follow, follow and
keep the promise I gave her.
The promise of meeting,
meeting her in the afterlife.

We were strangers that night.
I thought it wouldn't last.
But how wrong I was.
Not knowing that what feeling could do.
How they'd suddenly be there.
And somehow not go away.
Even when you're gone-
I fucking hate missing you so much.
Because I love you to hate you?

And maybe she was right.
Right about the way life was
but I still wouldn't want to
believe what she had said.
After all those lies
I didn't know what to believe anymore.
Didn't know whom to believe …
it felt like I didn't know
anything anymore.
And keep asking myself
over and over again:
why'd she lie to me?
Lie to me 'bout all those things?
Why, oh, why?
And the worst part?
I'd immediately believe her again,
again, over and over, again …

I wish I didn't miss you
I even wish I didn't love you
but I do
from the bottom of my heart
and I can't help it
can't help it to
love you and miss you so much
so much it hurts so bad.

How am I supposed to move on
if I didn't even get the chance
to tell you how I feel?
Tell me how – oh, wait,
you can't, you didn't even
reply to that letter, but still
I stand there every day
hoping for at least something:
a letter back or even you visiting?

This feeling of being empty
of being this shadow of myself …
will it go away?
The night you left …
it changed everything
or nothing?
I don't know.
I wish I knew.
Knew all the answers to those questions.
But I don't, wish I did.
Maybe if I didn't love you so much?

These words
all for you
presumably
you'll never read.
Wish you did
then you'd know
how I feel –
feel 'bout you.

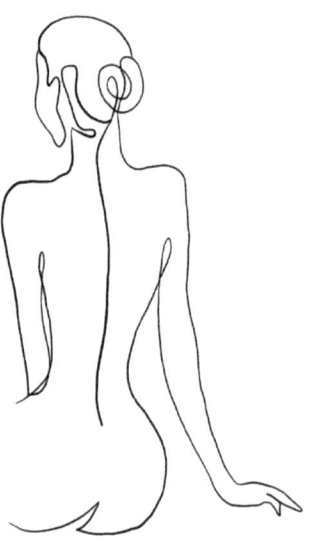

What if loving
meant hurting?
What if it
meant I was free
at the same time?
What if it
meant so many
damn things
at the same time?
What if I
really truly
loved you?
What if they
told me
I couldn't?
Couldn't love
love you …
I'd still do,
still love you
from the bottom of my heart.

Be my queen
and I'll be your king.
On the throne
right by your side.
Come with me, baby.
Just the two of us,
Reigning together.
Our wonderful garden
will be the
kingdom of our dreams-
Just trust me, dear,
have no fear,
I'll keep you safe,
keep you safe, keep you safe.
I promise.

Take me back,
back to the day we met.
At that riverbank.
Just you and me
and me and you.
Talking 'bout life, 'bout love,
'bout almost everything.
I wish I could
fall in love with you again
and I would like
to meet you again and again.
At that riverbank and
that lake that means
something special for me now.
Because of you.
Take me back,
back to that night I lay
in your strong-soft arms
where I felt safe and sound.
Take me back
to all those moments we had
because I love you.

Butterflies fly away
fly away from misery
from misery to brightness
to brightness from darkness.
From darkness she came
she came and fell so deep
fell so deep, deeply, madly in love
in love with that person
with that person that she thought
she thought could have saved her
saved her from all those demons
those demons that ate her soul
her soul from the inside
the inside broken like glass
like glass that's shattered all over
all over the world
the world that told her
told her she was enough
she was enough, but could not believe it
believe it that relied on others
on others so much that it was too late
too late … too late … too late …

I don't care
care 'bout what you say
what you feel ...
just wanted to tell you
that I love you ...

Fuck these feelings,
Fuck love!
The only thing I want to
is feel you and
forget about what the fuck
is going on around us.

Prisoner

Feels like
I'm this prisoner in my own head.
Tried to break free
But couldn't.
Could've cried for help
But didn't.
Waited for you in the rain
You never came.
Feels like
I'm drowning crying for help –
Too late!
I already took the ferryman's hand.
There's no way back
Not even when you're my Orpheus
And I'm your Eurydice …
We all know how the story ends.

Wishing well

She misses her world
bound to love
in this dark place down under
wouldn't want to let go
of what she has now
still wishing to go back
just once –
one last time
make sure all is well
one last goodbye
to fulfil her dreams in misery.

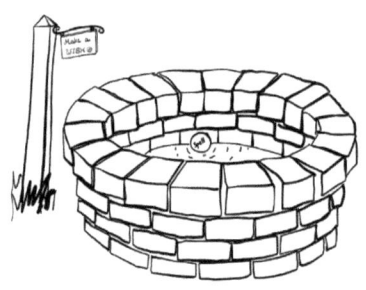

Wandering mind

And my mind wanders and wanders and wanders
Thinking 'bout you or something else?
Wish to be with you or
thoughts of me to be with you?
Want you to be here and
I go back to all those memories,
all those moments we had
when we were together
lying there thinking: will it last forever?
We didn't know
and still don't know –
I smile as my mind wanders
wanders to you and I wonder
wonder what these thoughts
would do with you.

Sleep sweet, my dear
'til morning comes
I'll hold you tight
right by my side
kiss you goodnight
when the moon rises
I may be gone for a while
be back before you wake
just sleep tight, darling,
when you need me
I'll be right by your side.

Feels like freedom, doesn't it?
I breathe in the fresh air
tickling my face
wind playing with my hair.
Breathing slow
but heartbeat's fast.
Spark in my eyes,
smile on my face.
I look at it in gaze
my mind wanders
and wanders, wanders, wanders
far, far away …
feels like home though so far away –
guess my heart's here
at this place, this city,
city I love.

I like thinking 'bout you,
my heart leaps up
thinking 'bout that smile
on your lovely face
when you look a me –
suddenly all the trouble's gone.

It rips my heart out to
see you like this …
standing there, lonely,
wish I could be right
by your side, but …
… I can't …
… too much time has passed,
I've been gone for too long.

Dreaming of soft warm kisses
hoping you'll be alright
water around us and
I see that smile upon your face.
Wish you were here
right by my side
holding my hand and
telling me everything's going to be alright.

In love she fell
caused by that spell
wish she didn't tell
where I'd find the wishing well.
I'd like to forget
and not regret
the wish I made for that bet
leaving her upset.
Love, all gone
for one last time withdrawn –
I wish I had never let her go
and did not just love her for the show.

Maybe I'm heartless.
But who said you weren't?
When you played and made me feel loved,
When I dreamed and you crushed
everything.
But how about that time you said:
'I love you, baby'
And then made my heart bleed,
bleed, and bleed, and bleed.
When you burned all the letters, I sent you.
When you burned the bridges down.
When you crushed my dream, my hopes, my
everything …
But I rose from the ashes.
I learned.
And now: I'll make you bleed.
I'll crush your dreams, your hopes, your
everything …

Sometimes I just
Want to get lost in your eyes
Cause I love, love, love you
So much until eternity …
… always and forever.

Empty streets
I feel so free
Life so blurry
feels loke I'm defying gravity
wish I could forget
the way you made me feel
oh, the streets so empty
I feel so free
the wish for you to be
right by my side.

she dreamed of paradise
a world where all the trouble would be gone
a world where she felt wanted
she dreamed and dreamed and dreamed
never wanting to wake up
and when she woke up
she still dreamed

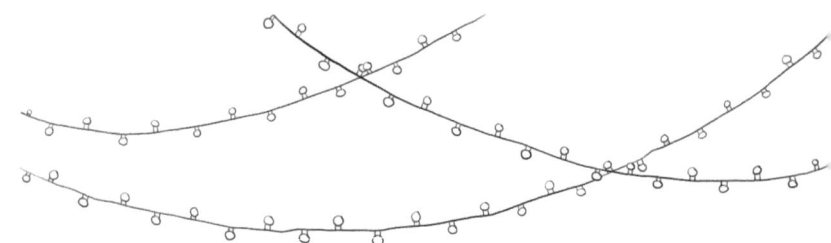

All these lights around us,
make me smile and
light up the whole world.
How it feels like,
you ask?
Like flying and dreaming.
I feel so free, so warm,
everyone I love
represented in these lights around us.

Body

Wish I could love my body,
the way you do.
But I don't.
Why, you ask?
Because, I say.
Why, you ask, again.
So many reasons, I reply.
Too many reasons
to fit in a lifetime.
Wish I could tell you.
Tell you how it feels like.
But I can't.
You wouldn't get it,
wouldn't understand.
Wish you could,
wish I could tell you more.
More about that pain
inside me.
But I can't.
Or maybe I won't –
it would hurt too much …

There's blood on my face
Drippin', droppin', flowin' …
my hand in yours
grippin', holdin' on until
I can't …
I can't do it anymore
living with this burden …
the burden of your head …
… your head in my hands and
blood all over the place –
fresh and warm blood.

How it feels like?
I don't know,
Don't know how to describe it.
You wonder why?
I wish it was easy to explain …
… surprise: it's not.
It's like I fall apart,
wanting two things, but
only be able to decide for one.
One would be being me,
living the life I want for my sake,
giving the best.
The other would be a shadow of me
living the life I want for their sake,
giving the best.
One would be with you,
the other without you.
One would mean losing them,
the other would mean losing you.
And in the end?
I'm stuck in between.
My heart tells me to go with you,
my brain to stay with them.
I'm torn, even though everything draws me to you.

I was busy thinking `bout you
seems like
I can't get you out of my head
Don't want to
get you out of there
keep your memory so close
so very close to my heart
can't get over the fact
I miss you so much
it even hurts
so bad and makes me cry
wish you were here
right by my side
right in my arms

Wish I could have loved you
the way you loved me
but I couldn't
something was holding me back
and that something …
… that something was me

The way love crushes your spirit
Like it was glass shattered into thousand pieces
That's how I feel right now
Shattered into thousands of pieces
So tired, so broken, so weak
All I think about is you
But you're gone
Not gone gone, but gone
Wish you were still here
Right by my side
I miss you
I miss you so much
More than I hate it
Hate it that I love you
Still love you …

sometimes it takes nothing
to make everything fall apart
walls shatter down
tears fall, hearts break
the bond that was never meant to end
suddenly stops existing
everything's gone
gone, gone, gone
it just falls apart
because the one person who held on the most
suddenly let's go and then
all's gone …

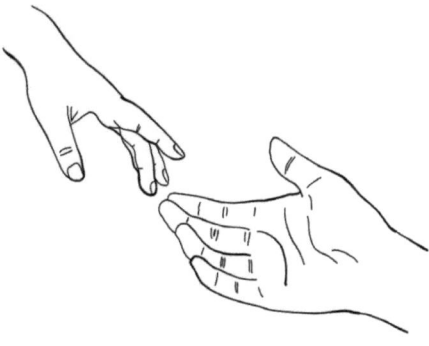

I just can't do it anymore
I give and I give and I give
give more and more,
but what do I get in return?
Do I get something in return?
I give more and more and more,
it drains me until
I'm not me anymore …
I'm not me,
I'm just this
empty shell of who I used to be …

Take it away
make it go away
this feeling
this pain around my heart
just make it go away
I can't do it anymore
I don't want it anymore
make it go away
please, make it go away
I don't wanna live anymore …

…

… I just can't …

Sometimes I feel overwhelmed
overwhelmed 'cause it's too much
all of it, everything
then I realise
it's not
all of it is in my head
in my mind
just me thriving for perfection
perfection expected from me
by everyone
I feel like it gets too much
I feel overwhelmed
just to realise:
it's just in my head
and I don't owe them anything.

Thought we'd find a way
a way out of everything
all of it.
We hate it so much
are full of anger
detest it.
But we're still here
stuck
stuck in the middle of nowhere.
Alone.
Without any loved ones.
Lost.
In this abandoned desert.
Lost and alone.

my mind's just a prison
I cannot get out of
lost in thoughts
lost in feels
I feel with my brain
think with my heart
survive is what I want to
crying for help
crying to be heard
even crying to be seen
it's just me and my mind
caught in there forever?

Sometimes I feel like I can barely breathe.
As if the air was getting thinner and thinner.
My eyes fill up with tears.
I feel like I'm screaming under water.
Louder and louder.
But no one can hear me.
People see me but their eyes pass by.
Passer-by in my life.
I try to reach out, but my hand reaches into the void.
I wish you could see me the way I was.
I wish you would see the real me.
I wish you would accept the real me.
I wish you would forget this silhouette,
 this ghost, of who you thought I was.
I wish, I wish, I wish.
I wish for many things.
Too many things.
What I mostly wish for:
to finally breathe again!

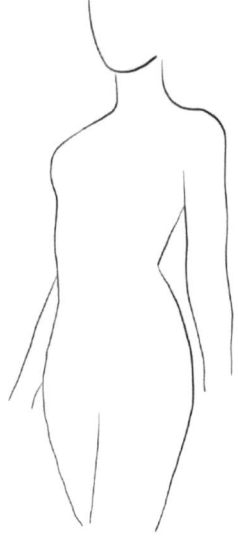

fucking dreams
from so deep below
deep dark thoughts
crawling up at night
taking over your sweet sleep
you try to wake up
try to move, try to escape
but you can't
you're paralysed
paralysed until
it's all over

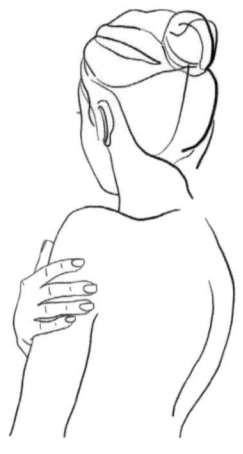

didn't think
that missing you
would be so hard
I've just realised
I'm paralysed
my soul's scarred
didn't think
that missing you
would be loving you
missing you and loving you
and loving you even more

all the tears in my eyes
wiped away the white little lies
despite my desperate tries
my love for you never dies
I wish to smother that flame
the one that carries your name
wish for the pain to end
just to be gone by the wind
but something's holding me back
just keeps me on the track
leading to you baby, only you, dear baby

loving you
meant hurting
but I'll do it again
again and again and again
all over and again
'cause I still love you
I love you, baby
I love you, I love you, I love you
I love you so much, baby
come and be with me
I wanna drink thine divine …

Imagine me and you, baby
we meet again
again in Paris
curled up in sheets
with red, red wine
your kisses and love all over me
'never let go', you say
'I'll never let go', I say
the sun starts to rise
our hands meet, again
I hold on, hold you tight
tight as I can
I look in your green eyes
the city is waking up
but for now: it's just you and me
me and you
imagine you and me, baby
your hand in mine, my hand in yours
it feels like eternity …
… maybe it is eternity
your eyes meet mine: you smile.

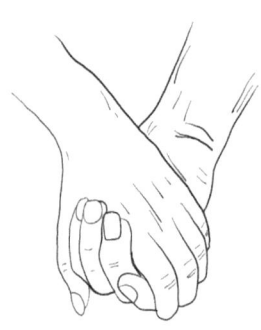

Why, you ask
Why not, I reply
you laugh
I love it
how you love
lovely dimples, the wrinkles in your eyes
you make me smile
your sweet, sweet face
your green, green eyes
I haven't seen you in months
I miss your face, your smile, …
… your everything
the way you talk, walk
the way you curl your lip
stick out your tongue when you concentrate
your laugh, your voice, your touch
so much longing
I wish you'd never let go
I miss you, so
I wrote this book for you
not my first love, but my last
never thought I'd fall so hard
longing for you, missing you
maybe you'll read this one day
or maybe not
it's out there, just for you
because I love you.

It's this field of memories I see
lost in the deep blue sea
lost in your green, green eyes
lost in the infinite skies.
I walk upon a field of dandelions
the wind slowly blows
carrying away my sweet, sweet love.
Dandelions fly far, far away
I make a wish, make thousands
feeling like a stray
waiting to go home to that place,
the place where my heart is …
… where, oh, where?
Where's my home? Where's my heart?
Home's where the heart is
is the heart where home is?
I see the deep blue sea, infinite skies
sun is setting on all of the lies
I see, I see, I see
finally, I see home. And heart. And home. And heart.
Your green, green eyes,
I see you and home and heart
I see you, your green, green eyes
and realise
I just set you free, 'cause birds are meant to fly
I cry
desperately cry and try and try and try
I try to fly
but I gave you my wings
left with longing, longing for hope, longing for love,
longing for green …
… longing for you.

I wish to go back
to that time in Paris
when everything was alright
when we lied together on that sofa
kissing while *Kiss the Boy* was playing
my memory's so vivid
still feeling the butterflies when thinking about you
I do it every day
thinking about you
and it even makes me miss you more
I cry, hot tears run down my cold cheeks
I feel like my heart's turning to stone
I don't see love anymore
I just feel the pain
the empty pain you left with me
why? To this day I ask myself, why?

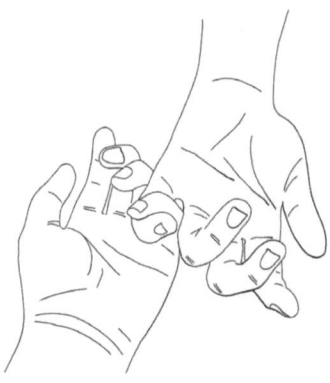

I cry and I try
woken up by my dreams
by my deepest screams
I try and I cry
Oh, the pain, the vain pain
I put myself into
I miss you
wish to break this chain
I stay awake at night
stargazing
slowly fading
into the light
I miss you
wish you'd knew
just got the cue
of how much I love you
It hurts so bad
I don't get mad
not at you
there's nothing I'd do
to hurt you
It's just so hard
so goddamn hard
I miss you and love you
miss you
love you
miss you, love you, miss you, love you
love you, hat you, love you more
love to hate you?
hate to love you?
I just miss and all I want to say is
I love you!

Who will fix my broken heart
it feels like I'm drowning,
heart's aching
you tore it out

it hurt so bad,
so, so bad
bad, bad, bad,

I wish I could go back
go back to that time I thought all was okay
it still is okay, isn't it?

I pretend that I'm fine
I act, I smile, I laugh
I pretend that I'm fine

I got out, meet new people
and yet, still thinking about you
always thinking about you

you're stuck
in my thoughts, in my head, in my dreams
I don't want to sleep, I can't sleep
it would hurt too much

seeing you there, seeing that everything was fine
or not, depends, sometimes it's just bad…
… but the worst thing?

Waking up to reality and knowing you're not here.
Not by my side, but holding her hand
I can't help it, it hurts
but I'm happy

I saw your shining eyes when you talked about her
the way your eyes always shine when you're passionate
I wish it was me, one of my deepest desires

but it's not me
it'll never be me
and that's okay

all I want is you to be okay
because that's love, isn't it?
Letting go and moving on?

I told myself I was okay
told everyone I was okay
even told your friends I was fine
turns out I'm not
since you've been gone
I feel empty all the way
the emptiness won't go away
maybe I'll find my way
but I can't see where to go
I don't see a way out
I only see you
every night in my dreams
I wish I was okay
but I'm not
I just wish you were here

You were a part of me
I felt you, I miss you
You belonged to me
Or I belonged to you
I felt you, I miss you
You were here for me
And I was there for you
Wanted to hold you, embrace you
I felt you, I miss you
You could have been here with me
Right by my side
We'd be playing and growing together
Dancing and singing side by side
I felt you, I miss you
Miss you so much
Almost making me cry, making me cry
I miss you so, so much
Wish you were here,
Wish I could hold you
Just one time, this one time
To hold you in my arms
I wish, I wish, I wish,
I felt you, I miss you
You were a part of me.

Always thought life was about more than everything
turns out I was wrong
more than everything, I asked myself
what could it be ...
so many different things,
many, many different things
looking for a definition all along
looking and searching when –
when the answer was lying in front of me
only thing was I could not see ...
what to believe
so many questions, no answers, many questions ...
the answer? where is it? is it here? there?
lying in front of me
me being lost
lost like a wanderer
like the lost astronaut building the house on the moon
I was looking for something
looking at it from a place the world forgot
forgot, forgot, forgot,
what did I forget? what was I looking for?
the answer lying in front of me
what answer? so many questions ...
I am looking for the answer, aren't I? am I?
tell me, tell me, tell me,
tell me, please!
life is about more than everything, right?
RIGHT?
I open my eyes
I see
I watch and wait
see for the first time: there it is, my answer, in front of me:
LOVE.

Thinking about my past life
about the moments we had together
lying together in your bed, in my bed
holding hands, kissing, dreaming
lying there looking into each other's eyes
talking about the future, about us
waking up next to you
slowly opening the eyes, closing them quickly
playing games
hot, warm, soft, gentle kisses
your arms around my waist
pulling me closer, holding me tight …
… sigh …
… all a past memory, slowly fading away
wanted to hold on, wanted you to stay
but it's my past life now
it's over now
last night you were in my dreams
last night I let you in again
last night I remembered again
the pain, how you hurt me, broke me
ripped my heart out, left me shattered in pieces
tiny broken shiny pieces
it was the last night in my past life
last night I let you in again
last night I remembered again
last night I let you hurt me again.

Reasons why I (still) love you

There are many things I'd name
your eyes, your face, your hands, your touch,
the way you smile, the way you frown …
the way you look while concentrating:
like a child, sticking its tongue out …
… in some moments even the lips pressed
on each other, a little forward as if
as if you were about to kiss –
but you're not – it's the way you concentrate-
The way you smile – awkwardly into the camera
little dimples on your face
you look away, put your hand on the camera
and yet I say:
'come on, one last photo, smile for me'
you roll your eyes, make a grimace –
then you smile for me …
It's the awkward poses you make
the finger guns, peace signs, your arms all over the place.
The awkward comments you make,
teasing me, making fun of what I just said –
in a good way though
I always complain about it, but I secretly like it
your dirty jokes, your nasty jokes, bad jokes
it's something I appreciate about you
I saw you in a dream, woke up and smiled.
It wasn't just one dream, tons of dreams
and I like each and everyone of them.
Your voice sometimes sends shivers down my spine
I like listening to you, the way you say my name
the way you tell all the stories …
… I could listen to you all night long-

And then there's the moment when you hold me
hold my hand, hug me, touch me, kiss me
pull me close to hold me tight
when we're in each other's arms and move slowly
slowly to the music that's playing
I remember one of the songs being *Heat Waves*
but that's not the only one
there are many songs that make me think of you
think of all our special moments
when I stood there at that train station
pulled you close to me and whispered
'I love you'
you whispered back:
'I love you too'
I cannot forget this day, leaving was hard
but we'd be reunited soon
and you'd be saying the following words
'missed you'
but whispering, as if you were breathing
only for my ear to hear.
There are so many things I'd like to tell you
so many thoughts I'd share with you
all the reasons why I love or
is it maybe all the reasons why I still love you?
There are so many reasons,
all the firsts, the first time we saw each other,
the first time our knees touched,
the first time we kissed, the first …
your smell, your style, your hair, your eyes,
just all of you and what comes with you.
But you're gone now.
Left me shattered in pieces, thousands of pieces
each and every one still loving you

loving you the way you are
I couldn't hate you, would never hate you
the pain you left, the emptiness
I miss you
miss you so much, it's unbearable
is it pain? Is it sadness?
it tears me apart from the inside
I always act like I'm fie
but I'm not
haven't been ever since you told me
'my heart's not in'
but mine is
more than 1000 percent
almost no day passes not thinking about you
I wake up in the middle of the night
I had this dream about you
where we had our happily ever after
where you didn't lie and truly said
that you love me
I sometimes think of what could have been
of all the promises we made
of all the futures and travels we talked about.
I feel so empty on the inside
and yet I feel so many things
there are so many things I'd like to say to you
I love you, I love you, I love you
so much and yet I'd always let you go
living with this haunting memory
with all this pain
acting like I'm fine
I want you to be happy
happy as the most wonderful person you are
of course I wish you would have stayed

of course I wish you had loved me
that you'd still loved me
there's this little part in me wishing for you
to come back and say it was all a mistake
but wouldn't I be a fool if had this dream?
Maybe I am a fool
a fool for loving a person who doesn't love me back
but even if the world ended tonight
even if the houses burnt down
even if everything exploded this moment
I'd still come to you and whisper like I did the first time
I love you.

Acknowledgements

This one is for all with the broken hearts. For everyone who has those dark thoughts. For all those who stayed up crying all night. For those who ended up with that someone. For those who got called being too emotional. For those who think, overthink. For those who feel. For those who love. For you because you are reading this. I love you.

I don't about you, but I've had my heart broken and my broken heart inspired these. Filled with pain, with feelings, with tears, with love. I remember vividly trying to forget, but I couldn't. Didn't want to. After a while it got easier. Easier, the more days passed. I didn't want to believe it in the beginning and here I am writing this. Normally you'd hear me say that my books are not about me. But this one's me. Purely me. My feelings and my love. And I want you to know. I have mixed feelings about this. I am scared what people are going to say about all of this. What people will think. But at the end of the, it's out there. My feelings are out there; I call the end of chapter 23.

That's why this book is called Thinking & Feeling. I wanted to take you through my thoughts and my feelings. Wanted to show you how the inside looks like. Wanted to tell you that you're not alone. That your feelings are valid no matter what anyone says.

At this point I want to thank my family and friends. Especially my friends. I feel like without them this book wouldn't exist. This one's for my besties, for my peeps on fire, for my booknerds, for my historians, for my queer royalty, for my cinematic team, for my dreamers... Thank you for being my support system!

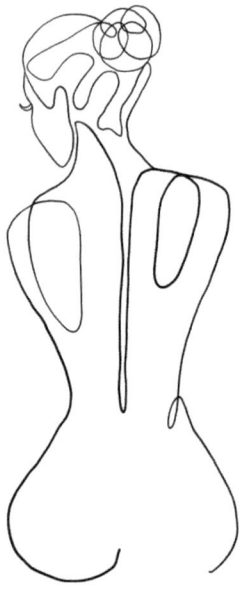